the cane groves of narmada river

the cane groves
of narmada river

erotic poems from old india

*translated from the sanskrit
and introduced by*

andrew schelling

city lights books
san francisco

Copyright © 1998 by Andrew Schelling
All Rights Reserved
10 9 8 7 6 5 4 3 2 1

Cover design: Rex Ray
Book design: Nancy J. Peters
Typography: Harvest Graphics

Library of Congress Cataloging-in-Publication Data

The cane groves of Narmada River : erotic poems from old India
    / translated from the Sanskrit by Andrew Schelling.
         p.   cm.
    Includes bibliographical references.
    ISBN 0-87286-346-8
    1. Erotic poetry, Sanskrit—Translations into English.
  2. Narmada River (India)—Poetry.   I. Schelling, Andrew.
PK4474.A3C36   1998
981'2100803538—dc21   98-35974
                                                                CIP

City Lights Books are available to bookstores through our
primary distributor: Subterranean Company, P. O. Box 160,
265 S. 5th St., Monroe, OR 97456. Tel: 541-847-5274. Toll-free
orders 800-274-7826. Fax: 541-847-6018. Our books are also
available through library jobbers and regional distributors.
For personal orders and catalogs, please write to City Lights
Books, 261 Columbus Avenue, San Francisco, CA 94133.
Visit our Web site: www.citylights.com

CITY LIGHTS BOOKS are edited by Lawrence Ferlinghetti and
Nancy J. Peters and published at the City Lights Bookstore,
261 Columbus Avenue, San Francisco, CA 94133.

ACKNOWLEDGMENTS

My gratitude to Professors Robert Goldman and Sally Sutherland Goldman of the University of California, Berkeley, for granting me access to the library reading room of the Department of South and Southeast Asian Languages and Literature. Thanks also to The Witter Bynner Foundation for Poetry, which gave me a 1995 translation grant to work on this book.

Many of these poems have been published in earlier versions. Grateful acknowledgment goes to the editors: *apex of the M, backwoods broadsides, Bombay Gin, Different Homeland, Gai (Tokyo), Grand Street, Japan Environment Monitor, longhouse, Many Mountains Moving, Pasta Poetics, Printed Matter (Tokyo), Sulfur, Talisman, Terra Nova,* and O Books.

CONTENTS

Introduction	vii
Poems from the *Sattasai* of King Hala	3
Poems from Sanskrit	33
Notes on Poets and Anthologies	71
Bibliography	83

INTRODUCTION

You hold in your hands a book drawn from the classical poetries of India. The earliest poems appear in an anthology compiled in the second century. The latest one translated reaches into the sixteenth century, although Sanskrit as a vital language for poetry disappeared from most of India by the eleventh or twelfth. I have taken the poems from what today are the best known anthologies, a handful of gathering places in which nearly all that survives of the old tradition is found. Technically, these short verses were called *khanda-kavya* — piecemeal or "fragmentary" poems. The term distinguishes them from *maha-kavya*, long poem-cycles of the court tradition, as well as from epic, drama, and religious verse. A few of the fragmentary lyrics may have originally served time as stanzas in a court epic, a few appear in plays, and some occur in small compilations that take on a life of their own. But whatever its origin, every *khanda-kavya* is a self-contained lyric, complete in itself.

Why the decision to select from various poets rather than focus on one? One obvious advantage is that it permits me to pick and choose, out of thousands, those poems I think particularly good. It also seems that anthologies, grouped into sections that focused on particular themes, were the way the poets themselves knew the work. I do not know if there ever existed in pre-modern India the approach that poets of the West have devised, to gather together the complete works of individual authors. If such a tradition developed, the books—bad luck—simply haven't survived eighteen centuries of monsoon rains, tropical insects, floods and fire, or the marauding armies (Rajput, Turkish and British) that swept the continent.

Sanskrit lyrics as they come down to us were carefully gathered and arranged into manuscript collections. Some of these anthologies contain over 4000 poems and distribute the poems into as many as a hundred thematic chapters. Invariably, there is a chapter for each of the seasons, six of them, as well as a large number that depict sexual love in its complex manifestations. When it comes to *khanda-kavya* lyrics I can think of only a few notable exceptions to the big anthology approach. The three books of poems attributed to Bhartrihari, a poet who lived in the seventh century, and the Amaru collection are first-rate work. These early collections are at least partly anthologies, not by any means a single author's complete works. And the *Amarushataka*, almost certainly an old compilation of high quality poems, was possibly circulated as an erotics handbook. A touching legend developed over the centuries gives history and personality to a King Amaru of Kashmir, and a few Indian scholars can't quite shake the conviction that this figure must have written the poems. However, the best poems in his book occur in other anthologies, either anonymously, or reliably attributed to authors of recognizable name. I go with the scholars who consider the large and historically later anthologies to give the best estimate of authorship for particular poems.

Despite the rather satisfying darkness that engulfs these poems — unanswered questions concerning who wrote them, when, or where — individuals of precise and likable personality emerge. Sometimes this happens on the basis of a single brief lyric. This is lucky for us, because very few poems by any one poet survive. Vidya (active ca. 650), the first and the finest among women poets who wrote in Sanskrit — whose eloquent erotic verse puts her in company with Ono no Komachi, Li Ch'ing-chao, or Sappho — is known by thirty brief lyrics. Her compatriot of a later era, the poetess Shilabhattarika, has a scant six. These are vivid enough, though, to put flesh on the poets. I like to imagine that had only a single poem of either's broken through the centuries, we might still know the unique passion that animated her.

The poetry of classical India begins not with Sanskrit, but in a literary vernacular of Maharashtra State. Probably in the second century C.E. a dynastic chieftain of considerable refinement named Hala assembled poems for an anthology known ever since as the *Sattasai* — Seven Hundred Songs. It is the earliest collection in India's classical tradition, a point of reference for all later poets and scholars. Hala's dynasty, the Satavahana, is remembered for the peerless Buddhist mural-paintings its artists brushed between the second century B.C.E.

and the sixth C.E. on the walls of the Ajanta Caves, not far from modern Bombay. But of Hala, scholars know nothing. Only his book remains. To various poems he attached the names of 278 poets, a small number of them women. These early bards wrote, or more likely recited (writing first arrives via merchant caravans in north India only a few centuries earlier), in an archaic but formal style. The poems take note of a tightly enclosed, nearly tribal world of small agricultural villages and pastoral settlements. In the nearby forests and hills dwell people that still live by the hunt.

Much in the *Sattasai* seems primitive. The standard verse form is a loose couplet, about thirty-two syllables. The poems would have been easily set to music and strike one as close to the cadence of folk song. Yet the refined themes of India's later poetry are fully present: love and the turning seasons, the moon and its phases, dark monsoon clouds, lightning and crickets, the Indian cuckoo, secret encounters by night, jasmine flowers, wind-tossed trees, inquisitive neighbors. Through it all, the many bittersweet flavors of romance.

At first striking glance you notice, in a poetry concerned mostly with romance, how much it is also a poetry of the outdoors. Our own arts of love and poetry have in the last decades largely drifted inside. But I think it worth lingering over the thought that for millennia the adherents of these intertwined arts, romance and poetry, practiced in forest groves, near rough mountain paths, in concealed meadows, and along river banks.

Rivers make great good sense. Everyone needs water, and before canals or aquaducts were built, or power-lines stretched over distances, towns almost always sprang up beside rivers. Merchants used rivers for shipment. Farmers and herdsmen required water as well — lots of it. Rivers and their tributary creeks offer cool trees, loam-rich soil, periodic flooding to nourish level farmland, swift transportation. And tall cane or wild grasses to lose yourself in. So lovers went down for water and slipped off a few moments where no one could see them. Not incidentally, India's patron goddess of poetry, Sarasvati, is long identified with several of India's rivers. Her name — Flowing One — catches the old connection.

There is an exact way in which the 700 poems of King Hala's *Sattasai* are celebrations of a particular watershed — the upland mountainous region north of Bombay. The hills are drained eastward, across the South Asian subcontinent, by Godavari River, which empties into the Bay of Bengal. Forests and riparian valleys provide the region's resources. The human who troubles him or herself over poetry may keep human factors in sight; but near the river the world of nature stays intimate. Cane groves with black bees, waterfowl, sunlight breaking on leaves, pastures and little grass hollows.

A few of the *Sattasai* poems wander northwards and cross a divide — another watershed — so the west-flowing Tapti and Narmada rivers also handsomely figure. Flocked with birds, blossoming trees, water buffalo, thatched villages, the poems would be unimaginable without India's great flowing waterways. Contemporary eyes read them as watershed poems.

During the thousand years that follow Hala's anthology, classical poetry occurs almost exclusively in Sanskrit. Its poets formed a professional guild. Unlike the *Sattasai* poets—whose names reveal a startling range of castes and occupations, from blacksmith to chieftain—most Sanskrit *kavi* (poets) were professional courtiers. Yet their work maintains the old familiarity with nature. In the second canto of his *Kavikanthabharanam*, a twelfth-century treatise on poetic training and practice, the poet Kshemendra gives counsel—

> With his own
> eyes a poet
> observes the shape of a leaf.
> He knows how to make
> people laugh
> and studies the nature of each living thing.
> The features of ocean and mountain,
> the movement of sun, moon and stars.
> His thoughts turn with the seasons.
> He travels among different people
> learning their landscapes,
> learning their languages.

Studies in natural history, the relaxed wit of a seasoned traveler, a bit of what today we call ethnography, and a cosmopolitan flair for language. Yet, of the precise texture of individual lives few facts can be found. What remain are the poems.

At the back of this book is a section of notes on the poets and anthologists, and what scant fact or anecdote I've managed to locate. I have translated a good many poems by women—poems credibly ascribed to women. But of the thousands of surviving Sanskrit lyrics, a large percentage have no credited name. Some of the best get ascribed in different books to different poets. Who wrote them? Women? That women were educated, and sometimes ranked highly as poets is clear. As far back as the seventh or eighth century B.C.E. the *Brihad-Aranyaka Upanishad* gives instruction on how a couple can ensure the birth of a learned daughter. (Curiously, it depends on the food ingested before intercourse.) Centuries later the *Kama Sutra* is also explicit on poetic training for men and women alike. Of sixty-four cultivated arts, twenty refer to poetry, another twenty to love.

None of the poems I've selected needs explanatory note. Consider this book a collaboration between the old bards, who now live in a "luminous body of words" (Bhartrihari's phrase), and a contemporary American poet. I have chosen poems that over twenty-odd years of study have proven durable. The translations are mostly quite literal—not inventions, versions, imitations. Yet Ernest Fenollosa's dictum, found by Ezra Pound among a batch of notes and published in 1918, still rings sharp. "The purpose of poetical translation is the poetry, not the verbal definitions in dictionaries." India's poetries confirm it. They have nothing obtusely Indian about them. They are not quaint, nor too tightly confined by old grammar. The settings, the specific flowers and trees, birds, animals, weather patterns—these belong to the South Asian subcontinent. But human emotions don't change much. Most of the poems could have been written yesterday, along one of North America's great rivers.

I've distributed the book into two sections. In the first are poems from King Hala's *Sattasai*. The second holds later poems, written in Sanskrit or a close dialect. Dates of composition are usually impossible to fix, but consider the Sanskrit poems to stand between the sixth and eleventh centuries.

It was traditional in ancient times to assemble poems into a *Shataka*—"a hundred" self-contained lyrics. Not tied up into narrative, not built on the personality of poets, not ordered too bluntly by theme. This way the poems echo and resonate off each other, creating distinctly audible swirls and patterns. Since to gather poems by the hundred fit the old poets' temper, I've followed their lead and compiled a *shataka*. As the old poet-anthologists would toss in a few extra for good luck, or to confound the literalist, so have I.

☆

It seems appropriate to add a quick word on watersheds, rivers, and a few of India's old places found in the poetry. I have watched the progress of India's monumental dams in the Narmada River basin with mounting concern. The Narmada, known to early poets as the Reva, figures in quite a few ancient poems. The enormous Sardar Sarovar Dam that taps the river is meant to provide power for India's future economy (a billion people crowded onto a not very large archipelago) — and to spring her into the twenty-first century, a ferocious industrial and electronic tiger of Asia. Built with funds from the World Bank, in the face of local and international protest, the Narmada Dam project has caused incalculable damage to forests, farmland, village economies, plant life and threatened animal species. It is also displacing tens of thousands of human residents, mostly underclass tribal people, locally referred to as "oustees." Vikram K. Akula writes of the project: "The poor bear the costs—ranging from the drowning of forests and agricultural lands to the salinization or waterlogging of surrounding lands. The government often does not give evictees adequate compensation."

And how do you compensate the loss to poetry, the possibly fatal blow whole cultures receive when the particular places known to their stories and poems disappear? Cane groves, where ancestors went to make love, and to make up a song to remember the moment? The village well where two youngsters first glimpsed each other, and having grown old invented a song their descendants still sing? Cultural heritage can't be quantified, nor can the intricate bioregions cultures arise from. That's why in the post-industrial world a few ecologists and poets are starting to take a new look at these incalculable resources and imagine a different economy of value. If you've ever met a friend under a canopy of leaves, or tasted love in the cool riparian shade by a creek, you know something of what it will look like. I doubt anyone has said it better than Shilabhattarika, back around the ninth century.

> Nights of jasmine & thunder,
> torn petals,
> wind in the tangled *kadamba* trees—
> nothing has changed.

Spring comes again and we've
simply grown older.
In the cane groves of Narmada River
he deflowered my
girlhood before we were
married.
And I grieve for those far-away nights
we played at love
by the water.

Andrew Schelling
April, 1998
Boulder, Colorado

Poems from the
Sattasai
of King Hala

It was like
touching the tenderest
dew-covered petals
the hundred intimate places she
guided my hands
Or was night just a dream?
Today she tosses
her head and won't
look at me

Makarandaka
Sattasai 1.23

Eyes closed
she imagines leading him
into her bed
she touches her own breasts adoringly
on her arms
the loose bangles

Anonymous
Sattasai 2.33

Forbidden they say
bad luck
completely indecent
but my heart yearns for that girl
flowered
with her first
menstrual blood

Anonymous
Sattasai 5.80

Night after night in the
rainy season
I'd push my way
through village mud to your door
the mud is no different today
but how
cold you have grown
how ungrateful

Anonymous
Sattasai 5.45

Many years later I
meet her again
but find no trace of beauty
no girlish wit I adored
What if I returned
to my childhood province
and saw in the
villages
no one I recognized?

Pravararaja
Sattasai 4.40

Stag and doe
hard short lives
ranging the forest for
water and grass
They don't
betray each other they're
loyal
till death

Apanagara
Sattasai 3.87

Wife of the traveler
head bent
placing a lamp by the window
What if tonight he comes home?
a thread of soot lifts
she blinks back
a tear

Brahmacharin
Sattasai 3.22

Don't go down
for flowers
to Godavari river
our village gods only ask
a handful of water in offering
petals crushed on a secret
lovebed
don't please them

Nandara
Sattasai 4.55

She conceals herself
where the forest is thickest
and waits for the sound—
dry leaves of
autumn
someone approaches

Madhya
Sattasai 4.65

Down in the hollow
two lovers flattened the grass
in the night
A boy stops his plough
along the impression—
troubled
by thoughts from a
previous life?

Nathahastin [?]
Sattasai 4.73

Catch hold of her
No evil spirit's
dropped into her womb
Her husband's
away and she's restless
The gathering rainclouds
drive her
into the night

Durddhara
Sattasai 4.86

She tells herself
he is coming
and night's first watch
flashes away like a shooting star
But in the hours
from midnight till dawn
the girl ages
a full year

Ardhra
Sattasai 4.85

Someone remembers
a lost love this
morning
and sings an old ballad
why must my
own heart be pierced
by a person who no longer
visits?

Keshava
Sattasai 4.81

Shiva tears off
Parvati's underclothes
during love
Playful delicate hands fold across
two of his eyes
the third eye she kisses
may it
protect you

Anonymous
Sattasai 5.55

Leaves from the back
gully
ankota leaves
stuck to the back of your skirt
brush them off girl
the household women will
see what you're
up to

Pandin
Sattasai 4.13

Pitch black
the night and I
dread it,
husband's off traveling—
Neighbor
stand watch with me
I fear what happens
in an empty
house

Abhaya
Sattasai 4.35

The pleasures
of a lamp blown out
of whispers and dares
caught
on the breath
a hundred sweet oaths
sealing the
under lip
Ah, and then stealing it
there in the dark

Vajradeva
Sattasai 4.33

Dusting her
body with
ash from the burning ground,
to join
the Order of Skulls—
but legs, arms,
too touched with pleasure,
sweating the ash off,
these are her own
lover's cinders

Hala
Sattasai 5.8

So long as his
flute sounds
I dance
A vine quavers and circles
the deeprooted tree
but my heart
is unsteady

Shashiprabha
Sattasai 4.4

Pierce
him with the dart tip
madden his glands
like mine
This life and next
O Love god
I'll fall where your
feet pass

Anonymous
Sattasai 5.41

O warrior's wife
your husband's drum skin
has struck
a terrible beat
love has brought doom
yet you keep
dancing

Anonymous
Sattasai 7.85

Sure they'll
gossip
even reprove us
it's only words
lie down beside me
you may be having your period
but I can't
sleep

Anonymous
Sattasai 6.29

Young men
used to slip this
wooden Ganesh
under my head for a pillow
today
cursing old age
I bow down before it

Anonymous
Sattasai 4.72

Must you weep
and turn your face from the moonlight
you should know love is
crooked
frail as the little
spines on a cucumber

Alaka
Sattasai 1.10

He has gone
and every moment
of every one of our nights
comes back to haunt me
Huge thunderclouds
are gathering over the village
they sound like the
drums
at a hanging

Kalyana
Sattasai 1.29

He gets up from
the mat
after we make love
and steps into the moonlight
Just for a moment
it's as though he's vanished into
some unimaginably
far off country

Makaranda
Sattasai 1.98

They asked if a few
threads of saffron had caught
on her breast
they laughed when she quickly
brushed
at the love scratch

Valaditya
Sattasai 2.45

No one to share a
quick glance
no one to lie with in bed
and whisper about pleasures or fears—
this hateful village
full of the
narrowest people
there's no one even to joke with

Meghanada
Sattasai 2.64

I have brought
many ox herds
and for a long time saved the great
bell collars
Tell Chandika the wrathful
that today I fasten them all
to the gates
of her temple

Satyaswamin
Sattasai 2.72

This morning he left as
the sun rose
I visit the temples
the city gates and the courtyards
I find them all
desolate

Amrita
Sattasai 2.90

Friends
have gone on before us
twisted stumps
stand alone in the desolate grove
Who would have thought youth could vanish?
Or love
have its roots cut?

Nirupama
Sattasai 3.32

What can I do?
we make love in the common position
he calls it sedate
but invent
something new
he asks where I
learnt it

Anonymous
Sattasai 5.76

In those days our village
had splendor,
young men came and went,
there was one girl
of the most
uncommon beauty
Tonight they speak of the old days
as though of a
legend
and I who've grown old
only listen

Anonymous
Sattasai 6.17

You say the whole village
is stingy
that no one gives alms to a pilgrim?
Traveler, you took my little
blossom and broke it
you should feel lucky
to get off
with your life

Anonymous
Sattasai 6.53

Cool thickets
leaves the color of clouds
cane groves breaking the sunlight—
but you've forgotten—
forgotten the River Narmada as well
how we washed
in it afterwards

Anonymous
Sattasai 6.99

I made love
to you in that particular way
for a taste
of your nectar
don't think me shameless
love is an art of
refinement
no one has trained me

Anonymous
Sattasai 7.61

Out in the fields
at dawn
he leans on his plow
studies the fresh green tracks
in the snow-white sesame flowers
and thinks of her
leaving
his bed before sun up

Anonymous
Sattasai 7.93

Crows wheel and fly up
from the riverbank
caw caw
they saw where the girl
was deflowered

Addhanda Raja
Sattasai 3.18

My bare legs flung apart after love
how could I
forget him
tasting each crease in my
body
as the climax
subsided

Shankara
Sattasai 5.13

Where has the sun gone?
have moon and stars
vanished?
Black clouds
mount the horizon
and like an astrologer's mark
a line of white
cranes

Anonymous
Sattasai 5.35

It's spring in the hills
of Malaya
and Mother in law
bars me from leaving the house
She must know
the fragrant *ankota* tree
luring me out
to the one
death worth dying

Anonymous
Sattasai 5.97

How many loves
we took
into those cane groves
the black bees also coming and going
But time dear
friend I'm afraid
has left on the riverbank
only dry stalks

Anonymous
Sattasai 5.22

Slipping before
dawn
from the bed of a half-awake friend—
others still sleeping—
if you
knew how it hurt
would your words be
so bitter?

Andhraraja
Sattasai 1.26

Midsummer day
leaf edges scorched by fierce sunlight
every tree in the forest
loud with
the rasp of a cricket

Anonymous
Sattasai 5.94

He searches the
evening sky
for a glimpse of the new moon
not seeing
raw crescent nailmarks
on his wife's pale
breast

Anonymous
Sattasai 6.70

You come to me
in secret
and I taste unimaginable pleasures
What transports do they know
who you
visit without the
deceit?

Adivaraha
Sattasai 1.85

Braids scattered,
earrings and necklaces tossing about,
a half-flying
half-divine creature
she mounts her
beloved

Anonymous
Sattasai 5.46

Even a sick old
buffalo
gives milk if the herdsman's
got practiced hands
but a consort whose
breasts
swell when she glimpses you
takes lifetimes of
merit

Anonymous
Sattasai 5.62

Please mother
get the cage
out of our wedding hut
this parrot has taught the whole village
to mimic our
love cries

Anonymous
Sattasai 6.52

Such poise in her gait
yet her face
tightens at each elegant step—
could a lover
have slid his nails in the night
between those dark
cool thighs?

Anonymous
Sattasai 5.63

Talking's no use
all that's written sounds trivial
do we alone
know how it hurts
to be separate?

Anonymous
Sattasai 6.71

You start awake
when the rooster crows
and urgently grip me
your own wife in your own house
as though dawn's caught you
in some
other girl's bed

Anonymous
Sattasai 6.82

Hear my words
near death
on the banks of Tapti River
my eyes
fall on the hidden refuge
in the rushes

Vidagdha
Sattasai 3.39

Poems from the

Sanskrit

and Related Vernacular Traditions

Have the gods cursed me?
At the gate
someone has planted a mango.
It's leaves are poison.
When the first fragrant bud unfolds
my womb begins
to itch madly for love.

Vikatanitamba

Dark smoking heavens,
dark earth,
turbulent clouds rippled with fire,
white petals strewn
on the grass.

Season of rain
season when people make
love through the night.
But a woman betrayed by her lover
has only
death for a refuge.

Vidya

Give me an edge
of the blanket
or take our boy on your lap.
I'm on bare dirt
husband
you've got some straw beneath you.
Thief who'd entered the hut
heard her talking
dropped his stolen tattered coat
over the child
went out to the night
and wept.

Anonymous
from the Paddhati (409), an anthology compiled
by Sharngadhara and dated 1363.

You act so contrite
slipping back
to cover my mouth with forced kisses
but excuses are
hollow.
Get your hands off my skirt.
Last night destroyed me.
I watched it pass
while you went to some other woman.
What brings you back
restless bee—
an old garland
flung to the ground?

Anonymous
from the Sringaratilaka

Tiny village asleep
black clouds rumbling up in the sky
a traveler
caught in soft rain
sings through his tears a song of desertion.
Nearby a girl
her lover off on a journey
forces her eyes
shut against difficult images.
Whole body
burning she lies there,
lies there and weeps.

Anonymous
from the Saduktikarnamrta (906)

Husband's still
inside the house
petitioning the gods for safe travel
& already
like ill-behaved monkeys
separation leaps
at the windows

Hemachandra's
Prakrit Grammar 423.3

Friend,
I warned you not to stay
angry for long
night is a
dream that vanishes
daybreak comes
quickly

Hemachandra's
Prakrit Grammar 330.2

How can I
sleep when my beloved's
in bed with me
how when he's absent?
For me the two
sleeps are annihilated
lost this
way or that

Hemachandra's
Grammar 418.1

Life on earth is
unsteady
death alone lasts forever, my love
Let go your pride
One day of anger
seems like a hundred
years of the gods

*Hemachandra's
Grammar 418.3*

They call him a lion
it injures
my pride
a lion
kills elephants
that go
unattended
my lover slaughters
the armed watchmen
as well

*Hemachandra's
Grammar 418.2*

If he and I
meet again
I'll give him something no
girl ever has,
whole
body coming and
going inside him
water in an earthenware
jug

*Hemachandra's
Grammar 396.4*

Nights of jasmine & thunder,
torn petals,
wind in the tangled *kadamba* trees—
nothing has changed.
Spring comes again and we've
simply grown older.
In the cane groves of Narmada River
he deflowered my
girlhood before we were
married.
And I grieve for those far-away nights
we played at love
by the water.

Shilabhattarika

You, my messenger
are a tender sprig
but I trust you with a secret dispatch.
Go to the wind-tossed forest
where that dark man
awaits me.
Black clouds trouble the heavens,
spring breezes stir and the heart
also stirs.
But go to him safely.
May the gods keep a close
watch
over your art.

Shilabhattarika

The Court Lady & Her Messenger

Why breathing hard?
>I ran quickly.

And your body hair bristling?
>A favorable answer—

Your braids have come loose.
>I fell at his feet.

But your skirt—
>Must be from going and returning so fast.

Sweat on your face? and so weak?
>The heat. And talking and talking.

Your lip, girl—the bruise—
what gave you that?

Shilabhattarika

Distasteful
a man with the stink of old age
who can't get his
thoughts off some girl—

—or a withered woman
tits sagging on a wrinkled old paunch
pulling a man
towards her bed.

Shilabhattarika and King Bhoja (?)

A difficult journey
but he's returned.
Tears, unsteady eyes—
she steps from the house to gaze at his face.
Then lifts a mouthful of palm leaf and thorn
to his camel,
with her skirt
wipes the desert dust
from its mane.

Keshata

Night
turbulent overhead clouds
& a ripple of thunder.
The traveler
stung with tears
sings of a far-away girl.
Oh traveling
is a kind of death,
the village people hear it,
lower their heads
      and quit talking.

Amarushataka 46

Through the whole night we slowly
made love,
body pressed against body,
cheek against cheek.
We spoke every thought that came into mind.
Lost in each other's arms
lost in words, we never noticed
dawn had come
      the night flown.

Bhavabhuti

I praise that silent
listener
her whole body bristling—
only a poet
linking words with ineluctable cadence
can touch
her entrails with fire.

Vidya

To a Warlord

Your flashing sword
has brought forth a child—
we call him Glory—
the wind
swirls up veils of dust to celebrate,
jackals lift their savage cry,
and your enemies
freed from the grim bonds of life
taste final
release.

Vidya

To Her Companion

Love's bond has broken,
gone is the
high heart's passion,
even truth seems a phantom
now that my lover walks before me
like any other man.
Vanished days of rapture
rise and return, dear friend, to haunt me,
and all I ask is
why this heart
doesn't break into a hundred
shards.

Vidya

When a lover
wrapping a fist in her
thick black braid
forces her with rough kisses—
Ah! savage words
pressed through that indignant
woman's teeth,
may they bring good
fortune
to all who suffer.

Vidya

Black swollen clouds
drench the far
forests with rain.
Scarlet *kadamba* petals toss on the storm.
In the foothills peacocks cry out
and make love and none of it
touches me.
It's when the lightning
flings her bright
veils like a rival woman—
a flood of
grief surges through.

Vidya

The red flesh-like filament
concealed in the
half-budded *kimshuka* flower—
faint crescent moon—
reminds me of
the love god's bow,
before he lifts it from its
        polished lacquer case.

Vidya

To Her Daughter

As children we crave
little boys
pubescent we hunger for youths
old we take elderly men.
It is a family custom.
But you like a penitent
pursue a whole
life with one husband.
Never, my daughter
has chastity
so stained our clan.

Vidya

Not knowing me,
Vidya,
dark as a blue lotus petal,
the critic Dandin
declared our goddess of verse-craft
   and learning entirely white.

Vidya

Where to
girl with bright thighs?
There's no moon tonight.

Out to my lover.

Not afraid, young in the darkness
to travel alone?

Can't you see—at my side
with lethal arrows the
love god?

Vikatanitamba

My lover
stepped towards the bed.
Somehow the skirt
clung to my hips
but the knot came undone by itself.
What can I say?
Nothing makes sense in his arms
not who I am
not who is taking me.
Is it me that comes?
is it him?

Vikatanitamba

You ignored
the turning seasons of love,
shook off advice
and treated your lover with
cold disregard.
Bright
coals of betrayal
gathered to your own bare breasts,
yet you cry out in rage
like a wild
animal wounded.

Vikatanitamba

Rainy nights
the city streets deserted
husband traveling
in a far-off land.
This is when Jaghanacapala rejoices
she likes to sleep
around.

Jaghanacapala

Darkness dissolving
let it go
pale moon rises so it rises.
Sister, all I know
is out there he is waiting.
Look at this house, its old roof,
this family—
a hundred ages of the gods it seems they've
held me back.
One more night like
this I ask
could death be worse?

Anonymous
Suktimuktavali 71.6

Whispers, deep kisses,
bodies perfumed with slippery oils,
betel nut
cooling the mouth.
To make unhurried love
the whole night before you.
Ah! but a hundred,
a thousand times sweeter the
quick and forbidden—
done in a moment
       gone like a thief.

Kutala

Love has grown crooked.
It hurts since you left.
This body gets thinner and thinner.
Days heap up
and I picture death keeping count.
Nobody touches me, darling,
I tremble like a green
       leaf on a twig.

Shilabhattarika

Those first days
of untempered love
my body and
your body were never apart.
The seasons turned.
You came to be my cherished lord,
I the desolate mistress.
Now you're the husband,
I'm the wife,
what will come when the year turns again?
Life must be cruel as a thunderbolt
if this is
where it ends.

Bhavadevi

Why are you thin?

Can't my body just be this way?

Covered with filth and cinders?

I cook for my grandparents in their little hut.

Do you ever think back
on the old days?

Never!
Then broke with a sob and
fell on
my chest.

Marula

To a Warlord

Your enemy's wife—
her body precious as the moon's corona,
eyes that trembled in a
moonlit face.
Oh she was proud.
And today her lovers
are the bandits she fled to for shelter.
High in the mountains
eating wild roots.

Gauri

Day is gone child,
today again
your cruel father sends no word.
The road has gone dark
let us sleep.

Anonymous
Subhasitavali 1106

Dug under earth's crust for drugs
to make me immortal.
Turned mountains to ash hunting alchemical
ore.
Then followed rivers
back to their source;
groveled, swallowed pride,
tried to get favor with kings.
Hooked on spells
hung up on weird arts
I wandered the charnel grounds—
but never shed craving—
never obtained a single pierced
cowrie shell.

Bhartrihari

Grieve, brother!
Great was the king with his
inner circle,
wizards who flanked him,
proud warriors, pale women.
Scribes and poets
setting it down into
books as it happened.
Bow to time—
a whole kingdom swept into memory—
now only legend.

Bhartrihari

Arrogant, spurring your high-strung
horse
past folk who travel
the road by foot.
It wasn't hard work or
good luck
brought you money.
You took your
sister, radiant with poise and good health,
pillaged the dowry and
      sold her.

Lakshmi Thakurani

No evil spirit
lurks in this wine.
And the night sky's no reason
to tremble.
Like ogress Rohini in pursuit of the moon
your wife
has taken to wandering.
Who will notice if you
take to bed
a new mistress?

Shita

Rest a moment
in the cool
shade of these tree-limbs.
I'd like a few words with you, traveler.
Up ahead the road
has no shade
not a pocket of water.
Rocks and sharp cliffs
make it
nearly impassable.

Anonymous
from the Subhasita-Ratnakosa (S.R.)(811), an
anthology compiled by Buddhist abbott Vidyakara
in the early twelfth century.

This village no longer
gives shelter
to travelers.
One night a young man
on a journey
lay down to sleep in our marriage tent.
He sang as he lay on the platform.
But a ripple of
thunder crossing the heavens
made him remember the one girl he'd loved.
What he did to himself—
and none of us stopped him—
was enough to destroy the
whole village.

Anonymous
S.R. 1661

Impenetrable clouds in the night,
deep constant rains
of the monsoon.
Pumpkin vines twisting
over the little hut's firmly thatched roof.
Who could be luckier?
Half asleep in the darkness
murmur of thunder and rain in his ears,
and a woman
tangled up in his arms
warm breasts against him.

Anonymous
S.R. 230

Hard rain
then soft wind,
a sky smoking with clouds.
Flashes of lightning
stroke a horizon
that's there and then not there.
Moon and stars vanished,
fragrant wet flowers,
darkness creaking with frogs.
And a solitary traveler?
can he get
through the night?

Yogeshvara

O troubled heart!
Here by the door of the hut
he fell at your feet.
And you denied him?
Now anger and vanity come into fruit.
Now love is banished.
Grief will be
your one refuge
through life.

Amarushataka 48

Calamity came to our region
with the cruel district
overlord.
Villages emptied.
A few ruined families
cling to degenerate homesteads.
Not a live blade of grass.
Not an uncrumbled wall.
But a mongoose pokes through the rubble.
And back in the trees
white pigeons are chattering.
They manage
to live without sorrow.

Anonymous
S.R. 1175

The children skinny as corpses
from hunger,
the indifferent relatives,
the water jug
patched up with tree gum—
these I can bear.
But that my wife in her old skirt
goes begging a needle
and has to stand with a broken smile
while the neighbor
abuses her—
this no one could take.

Anonymous
S.R. 1307

Somehow she
got through the day
anticipating
the hundred pleasures of night.
Her dear one's returned!
But now it's time to enter the bedchamber
and relatives
won't stop their dull conversation.
Mad with desire the girl finally cries
something bit me
shakes her skirt wildly
and knocks over
the lamp—

Amarushataka 86

My breasts at first
little buds
grew plump under your hands.
My speech
instructed by yours
lost its native simplicity.
What shall I do?
These arms
left my old nursemaid's neck
to creep around yours,
but you no longer
        set foot in the neighborhood.

Amarushataka 87

NOTES ON THE POETS AND ANTHOLOGIES

Part I: The Sattasai of King Hala.

I have been studying the anthology compiled by Hala for twenty years, and at each reading new poems catch me up with an immediacy that has no equal except for the candid poets of ancient Greece. The poems Hala selected are vivid, precise, witty, secular, tragic. Most are about sexual love.

King Hala appears by the best estimates to have lived about 200 C.E. He was a ruler of the Satavahana Dynasty, but aside from his anthology, simply called *Sattasai,* or Seven Hundred Poems, he has left no record. Nothing can be said of any of the poets that appear in his collection either. The poems, compiled in seven books of 100 verses each, are rendered in a *prakrit*, or literary vernacular, of old Maharashtra State. They predate the earliest verses from classical Sanskrit and establish the principal themes the later tradition found worth developing. Hala makes it clear at the outset that his collection will focus on love poems. He begins with three stanzas of invocation, the second of which shows old-time poets' consternation at pundits who have not tested theory against poetically lived experience.

> You'd think
> from their
> talk they were adepts

> at love
> Yet they never read
> never even listen
> to deathless
> Prakrit poetry

I find something remarkable here. Hala regarded poets as those people whose business it was to know love—know it in its intricate details—a position later stated in more explicit terms in Vatsyayana's famed *Kama Sutra*. Our own civilization is utterly confused about sexual intimacy. Hala's was not. To learn about the charms and torments of love, you consulted a book of poems.

Hala's dynasty, the Satavahana, is the same that painted the eloquent and infinitely tender Buddhist murals on the cave walls at Ajanta. Yet Hala's anthology is resolutely secular. The only Buddhist figure I can find in his collection is a young *bhikku*—patch-robe wandering mendicant—who seems ready to break the injunction of chastity when a pubescent village girl with bare midrift ladles some food into his begging bowl.

The poems approach love with a light touch and rarely swerve from the most tender, intimate, and at the same time circumspect approach. It is a particular tone, articulated half a millennium later as a poetic strategy by the seventh-century poet Dandin: to express an erotic idea directly is to be vulgar, to suggest it discretely is the mark of refinement. Some poems in the *Sattasai* act indirectly enough that later critics felt the need to elucidate.

> Hut of reeds
> tendrils
> off in the forest
> > birds
> > > scattering
> beating their wings
> upwards—
> young wife at her
> housework hears them
> arms and legs
> suddenly weak

Chaya

Commentators report that when the birds scatter the village girl (probably married quite young to a man she hardly knew) realizes her lover has arrived at their trysting place. Hence her quite physical response.

Two hundred seventy-eight separate poets, of whom eight are women, appear by name in Hala's anthology. This is a great number of poets. Few contemporary American anthologists would venture to include so many. It suggests a lively and considerable period for poetry. Hala claims he selected his 700 poems from one *koti*—ten million. Surely he exaggerates. Yet it tells us he put in his book only a fraction of what was available. In one verse Hala refers to himself as *kavivatsala*—"comrade of poets." But he was more than a comrade, more than a dynastic chieftain with poetic inclinations, more than a humble anthologizer. Forty of the poems are his own, some of them quite good, and he probably arranged or put into final shape many more. That hundreds of the poems go uncredited, including the final 200, raises a number of questions. Are they Hala's? Could women have written them, possibly courtesans at Hala's court? Were they uncredited folksongs gathered in rural villages, and committed to literary form by a capable poet or a committee? Part of the charm is that very likely we'll never know.

Part II: Sanskrit and Vernacular Poems

AMARUSHATAKA. The *Amarushataka* or Hundred Poems of Amaru is a collection of some of the finest poetry in Sanskrit. It dates from before the ninth century. Quite probably the poems accompanied or comprised a handbook of erotics. Some copies are illustrated with delicate and often explicit miniature paintings. Tradition ascribes the poems to an otherwise unknown Amaru or Amaruka, who is said to have been a king—perhaps of Kashmir. However, as many of the poems occur elsewhere and are credited to some of the tradition's best poets, Amaru is more likely the name of an anthologist.

Several old accounts in India tell how the fearsome religious reformer Shankara (ca. eighth century)—a sort of Luther of Hinduism—engaged an opponent in philosophical debate. He was roundly beating his rival in a publicly held contest when his opponent's wife stepped in. She silenced him with questions about sexual love, which Shankara, being celibate, could not answer. He asked for a hundred nights to prepare a response. Then through his powers of yoga he entered the body of Amaru, a recently deceased king of Kashmir whose corpse lay on the pyre awaiting cremation. The corpse woke to life. For a hundred nights in succession Shankara tasted love with Amaru's harem girls. During this time he memorialized his experiences in lyrics—one for each night of bittersweet pleasure. After the hundredth night had elapsed (and a few extra had been added for luck), Shankara returned to his own body, leaving Amaru's corpse to its fate. Returning to the hall of philosophical debate, he vanquished his female contestant. One presumes he later committed to writing the poems that had delivered his victory, and he must have signed them in gratitude with Amaru's name.

BHAVADEVI. Woman poet known only by three poems that occurr in various anthologies.

BHAVABHUTI. One of India's eminent dramatists and poets, probably active in the early eighth century. He was a brahmin from the southern town of Padmapura. The poem I've translated has been called the finest in Sanskrit by a number of critics. It occurs in the play *Uttararamacarita.* Jeffrey Masson recounts a story: When Bhavabhuti had finished writing his play, he rushed to his colleague the great dramatist and poet Kalidasa, who was absorbed in a chess game. Bhavabhuti read him the entire play aloud. Kalidasa never looked up from the chess board. When

Bhavabhuti finished, Kalidasa check-mated his opponent, turned to his friend, and declared the drama perfect—except for one superfluous *m*—in this verse. Bhavabhuti changed the word, and rendered the tone slightly more dry and reticent. I think it is this understatement that makes the poem so compelling.

BHARTRIHARI. Two figures known as Bhartrihari appear in India about the same time. One wrote an astute and elegant grammar, and figures prominently to this day in talk of linguistics. The other Bhartrihari was a poet, who left three hundred poems or a few more, grouped thematically into three books: A Book of Counsel, A Book of Romance, and A Book of Renunciation. Critics sometimes see the poems as representing three distinct periods in the poet's life, but it is more likely the folklore surrounding him holds the truth—a courtier or advisor to a king, Bhartrihari seven times swung between a scholar's position at court and the life of a bark-clad forest renunciant.

One tale recounts how the poet gave a treasured gift, some sort of enchanted amulet, to a courtesan he was wildly in love with. She however loved another man, and passed the gift on to him. In turn, this man loved some other girl and gave it to her. This girl adored Bhartrihari and, completing a terrible cycle, made the gift over to him. Seeing this circle of unreturned love, the vanities, false hopes, and absurdities, Bhartrihari quit the court life in disgust and retired to the forests for good.

The Chinese pilgrim I-ching, traveling India 671-695 and picking up legend as he could, considered linguist and poet the same man. I-ching also considered him a Buddhist, and the broodings on vanity and evanescence would seem to attest it. Yet certain poems speak of "moon-crested Shiva," and of wandering along rivers sacred to Hinduism. Translated into Dutch in 1651, into German in 1663, Bhartrihari was the first poet from India to cross into a European tongue. A fit tribute, if the poet was also the renowned scholar of language.

GAURI. Her poems occur in various late anthologies. Quite a few are panegyrics—"praise poems" written to a king, probably her patron and possibly her lover. She also wrote tributes to beautiful women, to breezes, and to hot summer days.

HEMACHANDRA (1088-1172). A man of enviably wide learning, he wrote books on philosophy, politics, religion, grammar, and history, as well as volumes of epic poetry and popular story. Being a devout Jain, he argued fiercely for the principal of *ahimsa*—nonviolence—and pleaded for alternatives to warfare. In the event of war, he recommended that ascetics, priests, civilians, the weak, and those who surrender be given pardon. He also condemned the use of what in his day were considered inhumane battle techniques and weapons of mass destruction—poisons, heated implements, large stones, and masses of earth dislodged against opposing forces. He was moreover a scientific grammarian. His famous grammar of Prakrit (vernacular) languages contains a large number of poems gathered to illustrate weird vernacular usage of words not derived from Sanskrit roots. A bow of the head to Hemachandra—his book preserves poems we'd otherwise not have. Sadly he gives names of no poets. I'm certain none of the poems are his, though. His interest was in collecting authentic examples of local usage. I doubt he bothered to edit or rewrite the poems he found.

JAGHANACAPALA has a permanent reputation based on the existence of just one poem. Her name is problematic—it literally means something like "shaking the pudendum" or more colloquially "sleeping around." The word *jaghanacapala* appears in the poem and is, moreover, the name given to the poem's formal meter. No one will ever know if some woman with such a name in fact existed—yet someone had to have written the poem.

KESHATA. I can find nothing about him except a tribute by the Bengali poet Yogeshvara that suggests high esteem for his verse, and that at one time he enjoyed a wide reputation.

KUTALA. Nothing known of her. In one anthology the poem is simply categorized as "words of an unfaithful woman (*asati*)."

LAKSHMI THAKURANI. Celebrated Queen of King Shivasimha of Mithila, who reigned in the fifteenth century. This is the most explicitly feminist poem I've seen in Sanskrit, by modern standards.

MARULA. Her name occurs in a verse by Dhanadadeva praising four Sanskrit women poets of the highest accomplishment.

Nothing else is known of her. This poem appears in several of the major anthologies.

SHILABHATTARIKA. Perhaps ninth century. Her poem *yah kaumara-harah* ("Nights of jasmine and thunder" in my translation) is to my mind one of the finest lyrics in Sanskrit. It appears in virtually every important anthology. Yet only six poems can be attributed to her, one of them the odd little collaboration credited to her and a King Bhoja, with whom she seems to have been on terms of considerable intimacy. Bhoja, both a poet and theorizer on poetry, constructed in his palace at Dhara an elaborate temple to poetry and learning. The temple has now become a mosque, but its central deity, Vag-devi (Speech Goddess), is housed in the British Museum. Perhaps Shila held a high courtesan's position at Bhoja's court. If so, this would place her in the eleventh century. Unfortunately, as with so many of India's early poets we have nothing conclusive about Shilabhattarika. Only a handful of poems to tell us, here lived a very considerable poet.

SHITA. I find just this one poem by her. It was written earlier than the tenth century.

VIDYA (or VIJJAKA). All agree that Vidya is the earliest and the finest of Sanskrit women poets. Or, if any woman wrote before her, the work hasn't survived. Vidya may have lived as early as the seventh century. Beyond that scant likelihood we have only speculation. In one poem she describes herself as "dark as the blue lotus petal," tempting critics to think she lived in the south, where, on the whole, the people are darker complexioned and skin tone can actually look blue. Rajashekhara, a much later poet, called her the "Kanarese Saraswati" (Saraswati: goddess of verse-craft; Kanara: district in South India). She wrote freely and convincingly of extramarital love, with a tenderness of expression I have not met elsewhere. Though only thirty poems survive, they convince me she is one of the planet's durable love poets. See my *Dropping the Bow: Poems from Ancient India* for other of her poems. Some Western scholar called Vidya "the Sappho of India," and the name stuck. Though Sappho lived 1200 years earlier, I like to imagine those two women sympathetically nodding their heads over one another's verse, and comparing sage accounts of amorous escapades.

VIKATANITAMBA. Known for her clean and simple style, free of complicated figures of speech, she lived no later than the early ninth century. In one curious poem she depicts her husband as coarse and illiterate, struggling in vain with Sanskrit pronunciation. If this was the case she must have led, as one observer remarked, a rather unhappy marriage. A later poet notes that Vikatanitamba was widowed and remarried.

YOGESHVARA. Bengali, who lived ca. 850-900. The scholar Daniel Ingalls has discussed in an essay a tendency among poets of Bengal to write what he calls "The Poetry of Village and Field." Yogeshvara is its notable practitioner—a man with an eye for nature and a heart for rural living. Most Sanskrit poets were urbane gentlemen and ladies, more preoccupied with affairs of the educated courtiers and courtesans they moved among than with rhythms of rural life. Yogeshvara by contrast writes in a poem, "My heart belongs to the meadows at the bend in the river . . . ."

SELECTED BIBLIOGRAPHY

I. Sanskrit Texts used for this book

Amarusatakam: A Centum of Ancient Love Lyrics of Amaruka. Edited by C.R. Devadhar. Motilal Banarsidass: Delhi, 1984.

Kavikanthabharana of Kshemendra. Edited by V.K. Lele. Motilal Banarsidass: Delhi, 1967.

The *Paddhati* of Sarngadhara. Edited by Peter Peterson. Government Central Book Depot: Bombay, 1888.

Prakrit Grammar of Hemachandra. The Eighth Chapter of his *Siddhahemasabdanusasana*. Edited by P.L. Vaidya. B.O.R.I.: Poona, 1958.

The Prakrit *Gatha-Saptasati*, Compiled by Satavahana King Hala. Edited by Radhogovinda Basak. The Asiatic Society: Calcutta, 1971.

Sanskrit Poetesses. Edited by J. B. Chaudhuri. Calcutta, 1941.

The *Subhasitaratnakosa*, Compiled by Vidyakara. Edited by D.D. Kosambi and V.V. Gokhale. Harvard University Press; Cambridge, 1957.

The *Subhasitavali* of Vallabhadeva. Edited by Peter Peterson and Pandit Durgaprasada. Bombay Sanskrit Series: Bombay, 1886.

Suktimuktavali of Jalhana. Edited by E. Krishnamacharya. University of Baroda Press: Baroda, 1938.

II. Translations from the Sanskrit and related vernaculars

Brough, John. *Poems from the Sanskrit*. Penguin Books: Baltimore, 1968. This book seems cranky at first glance since Brough translates into historic English-language verse forms, but he's chosen some good poems you won't easily find anywhere else.

Edgerton, Franklin and Eleanor. *The Cloud Messenger*. University of Michigan Press: Ann Arbor, 1964. Good translation of Kalidasa's most famous poem.

Heifetz, Hank. *The Origin of the Young God*. University of California: Berkeley, 1985. One of the most sustained erotic poems in any language, probably left unfinished at Kalidasa's death. Heifetz's translation supercedes all earlier versions. Excellent.

Ingalls, Daniel H.H. *An Anthology of Sanskrit Court Poetry.* Harvard University Press: Cambridge, 1965. The only complete translation into English of one of the massive Sanskrit anthologies, this one compiled in twelfth century Bengal by the Buddhist abbott Vidyakara. What makes this translation particularly useful is that Harvard University Press has separately published a carefully edited version of the original manuscript. Ingalls' introduction is still the best single account of classical Sanskrit poetry. See also his paperback selection, *Sanskrit Poetry from Vidyakara's Treasury* (Harvard University Press, 1968) with a revised introduction.

Jonston, E.H. *The Buddhacarita, or Acts of the Life of Buddha.* Motilal Banarsidass reprint: New Delhi, 1972. The famous account by Ashvaghosha, told in slow, courtly, ornate stanzas. This may be the earliest kavya or "high-art" poetry that has survived. An accurate but dull prose translation.

Koroche, Peter. *Once the Buddha was a Monkey: Aryashura's Jatakamala.* University of Chicago: Chicago, 1984. Aryashura's ornate poem about former births of the Buddha, in straightforward prose.

Lal, P. *Great Sanskrit Plays in Modern Translation.* New Directions: New York, 1964. Good, readable versions.

Merwin, W.S. and J. Moussaieff Masson. *The Peacock's Egg: Love Poems from Ancient India.* North Point Press: San Francisco, 1981. Fine collaboration of a poet with a scholar. Though a bit uneven in style, Merwin's translations are lively and audacious. Masson's introductory essay, along with commentary on each poem, gives crisp insight into the tradition. The selection of poems is unusual and brilliant— Masson took pains to scour out-of-the-way sources.

Miller, Barbara Stoller. *Bhartrihari: Poems.* Columbia University Press: New York, 1967. Barbara Miller remains, along with Daniel Ingalls, one of the luminaries of Sanskrit poetry in America. Her translations are accurate and unhampered by pretense. Bhartrihari, as she presents him, is one of India's most complex poets, a man who swung throughout his life between the heated pleasures of a position at court, and the cool reclusiveness of the forest-dwelling anchorite.

———*Phantasies of a Love Thief: The Caurapancashika Attributed to Bilhana.* Columbia University Press: New York, 1971. Tender interlocking poems of remembered love supposedly written by a Kashmiri man condemned to death for carrying on a secret love affair with the daughter of a local chieftain.

———*Love Song of the Dark Lord: Jayadeva's Gitagovinda.* Columbia University Press: New York, 1977. The last great Sanskrit poem that has survived. It is a dramatic cycle rehearsing the changing phases of love between Radha and Krishna. Though written by a refined scholar-poet, it gives a taste of what the oldest tradition must have been, when poetry, music, costume, theater and dance all joined ceremonially. Probably Miller's most heartfelt translation.

———, ed. *The Theater of Memory.* Columbia University Press: New York, 1984. Kalidasa's plays. Translations and essays by various scholars.

Nathan, Leonard. *The Transport of Love.* University of California Press: Berkeley, 1976. Good translation of Kalidasa's *Meghaduta*, though Edgerton's title *The Cloud Messenger* is better.

O'Flaherty, Wendy Doniger. *The Rig Veda.* Penguin: New York, 1981. Oldest known anthology of poetry in an Indo-European language, ca. 3500 years ago. Composed by a shamanic pastoral peoples with horse, cattle, and chariot; their poets were often inebriated on soma, a hallucinogenic beverage. These poems set the pattern for India's subsequent religious life. Excellent selection with notes by an able scholar.

Ray, David. *Not Far from the River.* Copper Canyon: Port Townsend, 1990. Versions of slightly more than half the 700 poems from Hala's *Sattasai*. Enjoyable, though Ray can wander pretty far from the originals.

Schelling, Andrew. *Dropping the Bow: Poems from Ancient India.* Broken Moon: Seattle, 1991.

III. Studies of Indian Poetry and Poets

Daumal, René. *RASA or Knowledge of the Self.* New Directions: New York, 1982. Translated by Louise Landes Levi. The best introduction to Sanskrit poetics. Daumal is the only European poet to have taken a serious look at Sanskrit's elegant poetic theories, and to see their significance for the modernist avant garde. Indispensible.

Dimock, Edward C., Jr. *The Place of the Hidden Moon.* University of Chicago Press: Chicago, 1966. Cross-cultural survey of the Bengali *sahajiya* movement, which regarded illicit sexual love as the supreme spiritual act and produced some of India's most rebellious, kabbalistic poetry. Very good.

————, ed. *The Literatures of India.* University of Chicago Press; Chicago, 1978. Fine survey by contemporary scholars. Covers the range of India's poetry, fiction, and film.

Gnoli, R. *Aesthetic Experience According to Abhinavagupta.* Serie Orientale Roma, No. 11, 2nd revised ed. Rome: Istituto Italiano per il Medio ed Estremo Oriente, 1956. A full translation with good commentary on the Kashmiri critic's view of *rasa*, the central concept in Sankrit poetics, which received its fullest treatment in Kashmir.

Goetz, Hermann. *Mira Bai, Her Life and Times.* Bharatiya Vidya Bhavan: Bombay, 1966. Curious account that mixes fact with wild speculation.

Hart, George, III. *The Poems of Ancient Tamil, Their Milieu and Their Sanskrit Counterparts.* University of California Press: Berkeley, 1975. Useful background on the poetry of classical Tamil, especially the shamanic context—full of sorcery and wild sexuality. He argues for a decisive influence on Sanskrit verse, which came later.

Ingalls, Daniel H.H., Jeffrey Moussaieff Masson, and M.V. Patwardhan. *The Dhvanyaloka of Anandavardhana with the Locana of Abhinavagupta.* Harvard University Press: Cambridge, 1990. Translation and study of two key poetics books. Contains poems not found anywhere else, all in precise and readable translation.

Keith, A. Berriedale. *A History of Sanskrit Literature.* Oxford University Press: London, 1920. The standard reference despite a dated and highly patronizing approach.

Lorenzen, David N. *Kabir Legends and Ananta-Das's Kabir Parachai.* SUNY Press: Albany, 1991. Good account of the hagiography of Kabir. Full of miracles and subversive mischief.

Raghavan, V. *Bhoja's Srngara Prakasa.* Third revised edition. Punarvasu: Madras, 1978. Compendious study of Sanskrit poetry's use of erotics.

Ranade, R.D. *Mysticism in India: The Poet-Saints of Maharashtra.*

SUNY Press: Albany, 1983. Reprint of a classic work—medieval mystics, visionary poets.

Schelling, Andrew. *The India Book: Essays and Translations from Indian Asia.* O Books: Oakland, 1993. India's poetries and music—with an eye out for politics, myth, environmentalism, and folklore.

Tharu, Susie and K. Lalita. *Women Writing in India, Vol. I: 600 B.C. to the Present.* The Feminist Press at the City University of New York: New York, 1991. Useful survey with an inexcusable gap—it bypasses the Sanskrit poets entirely. Criticism, politics, and biography interest the editors, who seem rather less interested in literature.

Zvelebil, Kamil. *The Smile of Murugan: On Tamil Literature of South India.* E.J. Brill: Leiden, 1973. Excellent. A thorough study of classical poetry from the South. Should be required reading for anyone concerned with natural history, environmental literacy, and poetics.

IV. Translations from languages other than Sanskrit

Ali, Ahmed. *The Golden Tradition: An Anthology of Urdu Poetry.* Columbia University Press: New York, 1973.

Alston, A.J. *The Devotional Poems of Mirabai.* Motilal Banarsidass: New Delhi, 1980. A scholar's versions of the 202 poems found in the standard edition of this rebel woman, whose songs are still widely sung on the streets of India, in temples, and by concert hall performers.

Bhattacharya, Deben. *Love Songs of Vidyapati.* Allen and Unwin: London, 1963. Erotic songs or religious allegory? Bhattacharya accomplished remarkable work, locating and translating Bengali poetry that was largely unknown in the West. Also recommended are his early field recordings of Indian music.

——————. *Love Songs of Chandidas: The Rebel Poet-Priest of Bengal.* Grove Press: New York, 1970. Chandidas, a priest, scandalized his village by falling in love with a low-caste washer-girl and singing the intimate details of their affair. Very good.

——————. *Songs of the Bards of Bengal.* Grove Press: New York, 1970. Street musicians of the crazy wisdom school. There are now some fine recordings on the market.

Bly, Robert. *The Kabir Book.* Beacon Press: Boston, 1975. Bly has popularized the poetry of Kabir, making the fifteenth-century social rebel and religious revolutionary the most widely known Indian poet to American readers.

Coomaraswamy, Ananda K. and Arun Sen. *Vidyapati.* Bharatiya Publishing House: Varanasi, 1979. Versions by a member of the old 'Bengali Renaissance.' Stately, almost biblical. Bhattacharya's translations are better, though, modern and more lively.

Coomaraswamy, Ananda K. *Thirty Songs from the Panjab and Kashmir.* Old Bourne Press: London, 1913. Includes musical notations and photographs of the singers.

Daniélou, Alain. *Shilappadikaram (The Ankle Bracelet).* New Directions: New York, 1965. Excellent translation of this dramatic Tamil *maha-kavya,* or long poem, in which a mistreated woman destroys a mighty kingdom with sorcery.

Dimock, Edward C., Jr. and Denise Levertov. *In Praise of Krishna, Songs from the Bengali.* University of Chicago: Chicago, 1967. Collaborations by a fine scholar and an excellent poet. This is *bhakti* or "devotional" poetry, arranged by the translators in the traditional cycle according to which Radha's longing and despair over Krishna mirror the human soul's changing relationship to God.

Elwin, Verrier. *Folk-songs of Chattisgarh.* Oxford University Press: London, 1946. Excellent. Now frequently anthologized, these songs were collected in tribal India by a man notable for both his ethnographic sensitivity and his literary talent. Also see his many other collections of tribal poetry.

Hart, George. *Poets of the Tamil Anthologies.* Princeton University Press: Princeton, 1979. Scholar's selection from the South Indian classical tradition. Very good.

Hawley, John Stratton and Mark Juergensmeyer. *Songs of the Saints of India.* Oxford University Press: New York, 1988. Profiles of six poets of North India with translations. Includes Kabir, Mirabai and Tulsidas.

Hess, Linda and Shukdev Singh. *The Bijak of Kabir.* North Point Press: San Francisco, 1983. Superb introductory essay and a readable translation of this major collection of Kabir's poetry. More reliable than Bly.

Nathan, Leonard and Clinton Seeley. *Grace and Mercy in Her Wild Hair.* Great Eastern Books: Boulder, 1982. Representative selection of Ramprasad Sen's wry, cantankerous poems of devotion and complaint to Kali, the Dark Mother.

Pound, Ezra. *Translations.* New Directions: New York, 1963. See his Kabir (pages 411-415). Though only five pages, a lovely and compelling rendition from "the English versions of Kali Mohan Ghosh." It baffles me that Pound scholars remain silent on them, and that anthologies of Asian poetry never include them. Though Pound presumably knew very little about Indian song, the music here is much more in keeping with the dignified eloquence of Kabir's music than the pop versions by Bly or the labored productions of the scholars.

Ramanujan, A.K. *Poems of Love and War From the Eight Anthologies and Ten Long Poems of Classical Tamil.* Columbia University Press: New York, 1985. Ramanujan's translations form a class of their own— impeccable scholarship and an easy verse style. This is his finest book. The society that produced these poems was tribal, ecstatic, and hungry for the glory of war; its poets utterly refined. There is an almost unbelievable balance struck here, unlike that of any other culture I've encountered, between tender eroticism and a hunger for the battlefield.

———— *Speaking of Shiva.* Penguin Classics: New York, 1973. Devotional poems by iconoclastic *sadhus*—many of whom still wander India today by the tens of thousands. Includes Mahadeviyakka, a fierce and irrepressible woman who refused to cover her genitals and, according to story, cowed the priests of her day.

———— *Hymns for the Drowning: Poems for Vishnu by Nammalvar.* Princeton University Press: Princeton, 1981. Haunting versions of this ninth-century South Indian visionary submerged in devotions to his Dark God.

Rhys Davids, Caroline. *Psalms of the Early Buddhists.* Pali Text Society: London, 1909. The *Theragatha* and *Therigatha*—songs of Buddha's disciples. Victorian-era translations of all the poetry, with useful notes.

Schelling, Andrew. *For Love of the Dark One: Songs of Mirabai.* Shambhala: Boston, 1993. Translation of eighty songs, with annotated discography of available recordings.

Schelling, Andrew and Anne Waldman. *Songs of the Sons and Daughters of Buddha.* Shambhala: Boston, 1996. Poems of the early Buddhist elders, drawn from the *Theragatha* and *Therigatha.*

Tagore, Rabindrinath. *Gitanjali.* MacMillan and Company: New York, 1913. The Nobel Prize winning book by modern Bengal's celebrated poet, singer, novelist, and educator. Introduction by W. B. Yeats.

Tagore, Rabindrinath and Evelyn Underhill. *One Hundred Poems of Kabir.* MacMillan and Company: New York, 1915. The book Robert Bly drew on for his Americanized versions.

Vaudeville, Charlotte. *Kabir.* Clarendon Press: Oxford, 1974. Excellent study with abundantly footnoted translations by the esteemed French scholar. Useful in particular for accounts of *ulatbamshi*—coded, "upside down" or initiatory language used by trickster Tantric poets.

CITY LIGHTS PUBLICATIONS

Acosta, Juvenal, ed. LIGHT FROM A NEARBY WINDOW: Contemporary Mexican Poetry
Alberti, Rafael. CONCERNING THE ANGELS
Alcalay, Ammiel, ed. KEYS TO THE GARDEN: New Israeli Writing
Allen, Roberta. AMAZON DREAM
Angulo de, G. & J. JAIME IN TAOS
Angulo, Jaime de. INDIANS IN OVERALLS
Artaud, Antonin. ARTAUD ANTHOLOGY
Barker, Molly. SECRET LANGUAGE
Bataille, Georges. EROTISM: Death and Sensuality
Bataille, Georges. THE IMPOSSIBLE
Bataille, Georges. STORY OF THE EYE
Bataille, Georges. THE TEARS OF EROS
Baudelaire, Charles. TWENTY PROSE POEMS
Blake, N., Rinder, L., & A. Scholder, eds. IN A DIFFERENT LIGHT: Visual Culture, Sexual Culture, Queer Practice
Blanco, Alberto. DAWN OF THE SENSES: Selected Poems
Bowles, Paul. A HUNDRED CAMELS IN THE COURTYARD
Breton, André. ANTHOLOGY OF BLACK HUMOR
Bramly, Serge. MACUMBA: The Teachings of Maria-José, Mother of the Gods
Brook, James, Chris Carlsson, Nancy J. Peters eds. RECLAIMING SAN FRANCISCO: History Politics Culture
Brook, James & Iain A. Boal. RESISTING THE VIRTUAL LIFE: Culture and Politics of Information
Broughton, James. COMING UNBUTTONED
Broughton, James. MAKING LIGHT OF IT
Brown, Rebecca. ANNIE OAKLEY'S GIRL
Brown, Rebecca. THE DOGS
Brown, Rebecca. THE TERRIBLE GIRLS
Bukowski, Charles. THE MOST BEAUTIFUL WOMAN IN TOWN
Bukowski, Charles. NOTES OF A DIRTY OLD MAN
Bukowski, Charles. TALES OF ORDINARY MADNESS
Burroughs, William S. THE BURROUGHS FILE
Burroughs, William S. THE YAGE LETTERS
Campana, Dino. ORPHIC SONGS
Cassady, Neal. THE FIRST THIRD
Chin, Sara. BELOW THE LINE
Churchill, Ward. FANTASIES OF THE MASTER RACE
Churchill, Ward. A LITTLE MATTER OF GENOCIDE

CITY LIGHTS REVIEW #3: Media and Propaganda
CITY LIGHTS REVIEW #4: Literature / Politics / Ecology
Cocteau, Jean. THE WHITE BOOK (LE LIVRE BLANC)
Cornford, Adam. ANIMATIONS
Cortázar, Julio. SAVE TWILIGHT
Corso, Gregory. GASOLINE
Cuadros, Gil. CITY OF GOD
Daumal, René. THE POWERS OF THE WORD
David-Neel, Alexandra. SECRET ORAL TEACHINGS IN TIBETAN BUDDHIST SECTS
Deleuze, Gilles. SPINOZA: Practical Philosophy
Dick, Leslie. KICKING
Dick, Leslie. WITHOUT FALLING
di Prima, Diane. PIECES OF A SONG: Selected Poems
Doolittle, Hilda (H.D.). NOTES ON THOUGHT & VISION
Ducornet, Rikki. ENTERING FIRE
Eberhardt, Isabelle. DEPARTURES: Selected Writings
Eberhardt, Isabelle. THE OBLIVION SEEKERS
Eidus, Janice. VITO LOVES GERALDINE
Eidus, Janice. URBAN BLISS
Ferlinghetti, L. ed. CITY LIGHTS POCKET POETS ANTHOLOGY
Ferlinghetti, L., ed. ENDS & BEGINNINGS (City Lights Review #6)
Ferlinghetti, L. PICTURES OF THE GONE WORLD
Finley, Karen. SHOCK TREATMENT
Ford, Charles Henri. OUT OF THE LABYRINTH: Selected Poems
Franzen, Cola, transl. POEMS OF ARAB ANDALUSIA
García Lorca, Federico. BARBAROUS NIGHTS: Legends & Plays
García Lorca, Federico. ODE TO WALT WHITMAN & OTHER POEMS
García Lorca, Federico. POEM OF THE DEEP SONG
Garon, Paul. BLUES & THE POETIC SPIRIT
Gil de Biedma, Jaime. LONGING: SELECTED POEMS
Ginsberg, Allen. THE FALL OF AMERICA
Ginsberg, Allen. HOWL & OTHER POEMS
Ginsberg, Allen. KADDISH & OTHER POEMS
Ginsberg, Allen. MIND BREATHS
Ginsberg, Allen. PLANET NEWS
Ginsberg, Allen. PLUTONIAN ODE
Ginsberg, Allen. REALITY SANDWICHES
Goethe, J. W. von. TALES FOR TRANSFORMATION
Gómez-Peña, Guillermo. THE NEW WORLD BORDER
Goytisolo, Juan. THE MARX FAMILY SAGA
Harryman, Carla. THERE NEVER WAS A ROSE WITHOUT A THORN
Heider, Ulrike. ANARCHISM: Left Right & Green

Herron, Don. THE DASHIELL HAMMETT TOUR: A Guidebook
Higman, Perry, tr. LOVE POEMS FROM SPAIN AND SPANISH AMERICA
Hinojosa, Francisco. HECTIC ETHICS
Jaffe, Harold. EROS: ANTI-EROS
Jenkins, Edith. AGAINST A FIELD SINISTER
Katzenberger, Elaine, ed. FIRST WORLD, HA HA HA!: The Zapatista Challenge
Kerouac, Jack. BOOK OF DREAMS
Kerouac, Jack. POMES ALL SIZES
Kerouac, Jack. SCATTERED POEMS
Kerouac, Jack. SCRIPTURE OF THE GOLDEN ETERNITY
Lacarrière, Jacques. THE GNOSTICS
La Duke, Betty. COMPAÑERAS
La Loca. ADVENTURES ON THE ISLE OF ADOLESCENCE
Lamantia, Philip. BED OF SPHINXES: SELECTED POEMS
Lamantia, Philip. MEADOWLARK WEST
Laughlin, James. SELECTED POEMS: 1935–1985
Laure. THE COLLECTED WRITINGS
Le Brun, Annie. SADE: On the Brink of the Abyss
Mackey, Nathaniel. SCHOOL OF UDHRA
Mackey, Nathaniel. WHATSAID SERIF
Masereel, Frans. PASSIONATE JOURNEY
Mayakovsky, Vladimir. LISTEN! EARLY POEMS
Mehmedinovic, Semezdin. SARAJEVO BLUES
Morgan, William. BEAT GENERATION IN NEW YORK
Mrabet, Mohammed. THE BOY WHO SET THE FIRE
Mrabet, Mohammed. THE LEMON
Mrabet, Mohammed. LOVE WITH A FEW HAIRS
Mrabet, Mohammed. M'HASHISH
Murguía, A. & B. Paschke, eds. VOLCAN: Poems from Central America
Nadir, Shams. THE ASTROLABE OF THE SEA
Parenti, Michael. AGAINST EMPIRE
Parenti, Michael. AMERICA BESIEGED
Parenti, Michael. BLACKSHIRTS & REDS
Parenti, Michael. DIRTY TRUTHS
Pasolini, Pier Paolo. ROMAN POEMS
Pessoa, Fernando. ALWAYS ASTONISHED
Pessoa, Fernando. POEMS
Peters, Nancy J., ed. WAR AFTER WAR (City Lights Review #5)
Poe, Edgar Allan. THE UNKNOWN POE
Porta, Antonio. KISSES FROM ANOTHER DREAM
Prévert, Jacques. PAROLES
Purdy, James. THE CANDLES OF YOUR EYES

Purdy, James. GARMENTS THE LIVING WEAR
Purdy, James. IN A SHALLOW GRAVE
Purdy, James. OUT WITH THE STARS
Rachlin, Nahid. THE HEART'S DESIRE
Rachlin, Nahid. MARRIED TO A STRANGER
Rachlin, Nahid. VEILS: SHORT STORIES
Reed, Jeremy. DELIRIUM: An Interpretation of Arthur Rimbaud
Reed, Jeremy. RED-HAIRED ANDROID
Rey Rosa, Rodrigo. THE BEGGAR'S KNIFE
Rey Rosa, Rodrigo. DUST ON HER TONGUE
Rigaud, Milo. SECRETS OF VOODOO
Ross, Dorien. RETURNING TO A
Ruy Sánchez, Alberto. MOGADOR
Saadawi, Nawal El. MEMOIRS OF A WOMAN DOCTOR
Sawyer-Lauçanno, Christopher. THE CONTINUAL PILGRIMAGE: American Writers in Paris 1944-1960
Sawyer-Lauçanno, Christopher, transl. THE DESTRUCTION OF THE JAGUAR
Schelling, Andrew, tr. THE CANE GROVES OF NARMADA RIVER
Scholder, Amy, ed. CRITICAL CONDITION: Women on the Edge of Violence
Sclauzero, Mariarosa. MARLENE
Serge, Victor. RESISTANCE
Shepard, Sam. MOTEL CHRONICLES
Shepard, Sam. FOOL FOR LOVE & THE SAD LAMENT OF PECOS BILL
Smith, Michael. IT A COME
Snyder, Gary. THE OLD WAYS
Solnit, Rebecca. SECRET EXHIBITION: Six California Artists
Sussler, Betsy, ed. BOMB: INTERVIEWS
Takahashi, Mutsuo. SLEEPING SINNING FALLING
Turyn, Anne, ed. TOP TOP STORIES
Tutuola, Amos. SIMBI & THE SATYR OF THE DARK JUNGLE
Ullman, Ellen. CLOSE TO THE MACHINE: Technophilia and Its Discontents
Valaoritis, Nanos. MY AFTERLIFE GUARANTEED
VandenBroeck, André. BREAKING THROUGH
Vega, Janine Pommy. TRACKING THE SERPENT
Veltri, George. NICE BOY
Waldman, Anne. FAST SPEAKING WOMAN
Wilson, Colin. POETRY AND MYSTICISM
Wilson, Peter Lamborn. PLOUGHING THE CLOUDS
Wilson, Peter Lamborn. SACRED DRIFT
Wynne, John. THE OTHER WORLD
Zamora, Daisy. RIVERBED OF MEMORY